Sight Words

Level D

55 more words

you need to know

to be a successful reader

Written by Shannon Keeley • Illustrated by Rémy Simard

Flash Kids

ISBN-13: 978-1-4114-0494-6
ISBN-10: 1-4114-0494-7

For more information please visit *www.flashkidsbooks.com*
Please submit changes or report errors to *www.flashkidsbooks.com/errors*

Printed and bound in China

Spark Publishing
120 Fifth Avenue
New York, NY 10011

Dear Parent,

Every time your child reads a text, 50–75% of the words he or she encounters are from the Dolch Sight Word List. The Dolch Sight Word List is a core group of 220 common words that are repeated frequently in reading material. Children need extra practice learning these words, many of which can't be represented by simple pictures. Often, these sight words do not follow regular spelling rules and cannot be "sounded out." So, learning to immediately recognize these words "at sight" is a critical skill for fluent reading. This is the fourth book in a series that covers all 220 Dolch sight words. The 55 words covered in this book are listed below. The activities in this book offer lots of practice with tracing and writing, as well as fun word puzzles and games. Your child can color the pictures, laugh at the funny characters, and enjoy learning about sight words.

The sight words included in this book are:

about	cut	hold	never	their
always	done	hot	only	today
around	draw	hurt	pick	together
because	drink	if	seven	try
before	eight	keep	shall	upon
better	fall	kind	show	us
both	far	laugh	sing	which
bring	fast	light	six	wish
call	full	long	small	work
carry	got	much	start	would
clean	grow	myself	ten	write

 **try**

say the word try aloud as you trace it.

try

Now practice writing the word once on each line.

try

try

try

try

I'll try a bite.

Keep on Track

Look for the word try in each track. Circle it each time you see it. Then count the number of circled words in each track and write it in the sign.

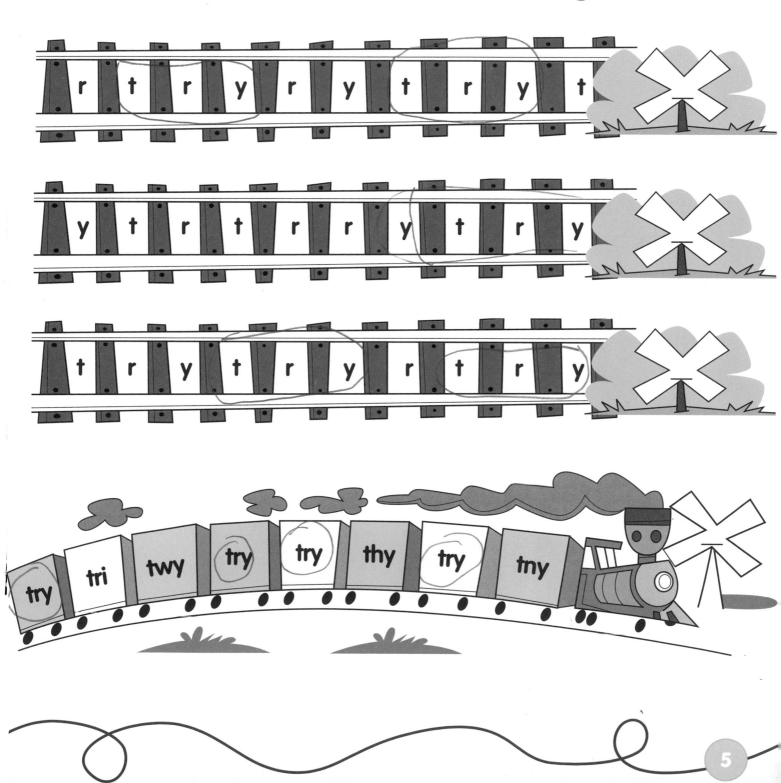

r t r y r y t r y t

y t r t r r r y t r y

t r y t r y r t r y

try tri twy try try thy try tny

 **better** **say the word better aloud as you trace it.**

b

better

Now practice writing the word once on each line.

better

better

better

better

I like apples better than oranges.

Word Watch

Circle the birds that have the word **better** inside.

 **say the word sing aloud as you trace it.**

sing

Now practice writing the word once on each line.

sing

sing

sing

Let's _____ a song.

Crack the Code

The word **sing** is hidden once in each column. Find the word and circle the letters. Then use the code to complete the riddle below.

n	**1: h**	s	**1: c**	s	**1: d**
g	**2: c**	i	**2: l**	n	**2: o**
s	**3: l**	n	**3: e**	g	**3: i**
i	**4: a**	g	**4: a**	i	**4: f**
s	**5: n**	s	**5: b**	s	**5: h**
i	**6: g**	i	**6: p**	g	**6: u**
n	**7: e**	g	**7: f**	i	**7: r**
g	**8: t**	n	**8: i**	g	**8: g**
i	**9: y**	i	**9: o**	s	**9: a**
s	**10: e**	n	**10: v**	i	**10: w**
n	**11: t**	g	**11: r**	n	**11: a**
g	**12: h**	s	**12: y**	g	**12: y**

Why did the burglar take a shower?

He wanted to make a $\underset{1}{G} \; \underset{2}{d} \; \underset{3}{e} \; \underset{4}{g} \; \underset{5}{n}$

$\underset{6}{g} \; \underset{7}{e} \; \underset{8}{t} \; \underset{9}{a} \; \underset{10}{w} \; \underset{11}{a} \; \underset{12}{y}$!

 **Say the word ten aloud as you trace it.**

ten

Now practice writing the word once on each line.

I have _____ fingers.

Target Words

Circle the words that have **ten** hidden inside.
Underline the letters **t-e-n** in each circled word.

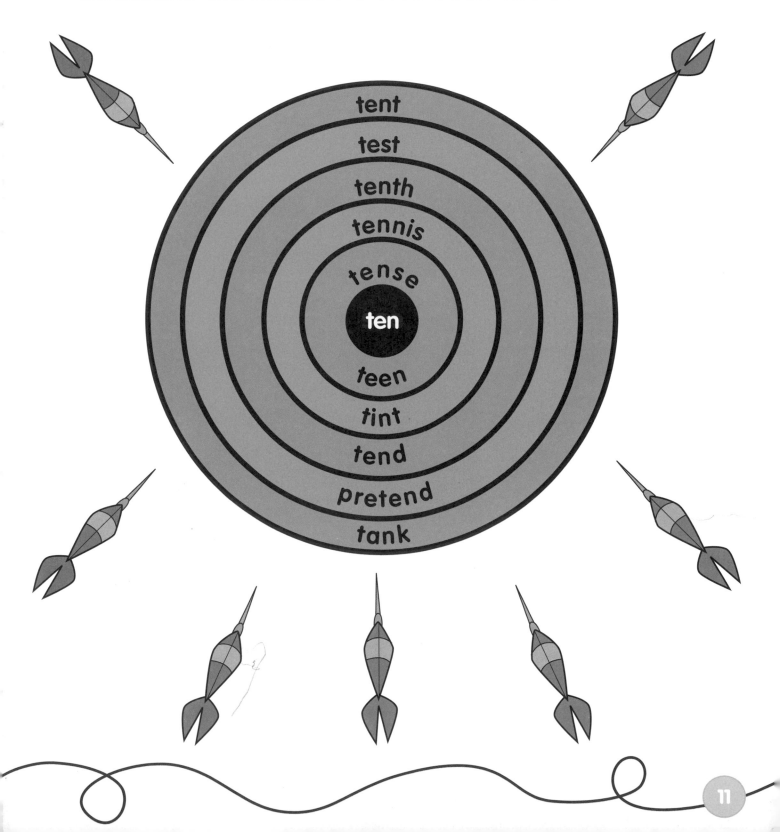

tent
test
tenth
tennis
tense
ten
teen
tint
tend
pretend
tank

 **Say the word us aloud as you trace it.**

us

Now practice writing the word once on each line.

This gift is for _____.

Pen Pals

Circle the word **us** every time it appears in the letters. Count how many circled words are in each letter, and write the number in the box. Find out which pen pal used the word **us** more.

Dear Alex,

I hope you can visit me this summer. There are so many things for us to do. My dad will make us pancakes every day. Our tree house is big enough for us to sleep in. You can stay with us as long as you want!

Sincerely,

Justin

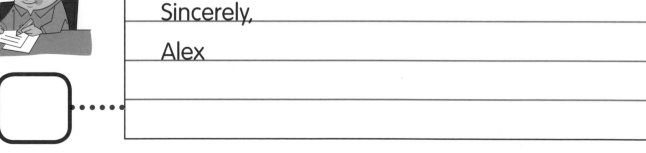

Dear Justin,

You've planned a lot of fun things for us! My parents want you to come camping with us. They will take us to the mountains. There is a tent just for us. Call us and let us know if you can come.

Sincerely,

Alex

Review: Crossword Puzzle!

Use the sentence clues below to solve the crossword puzzle.

try   better   sing   ten   us

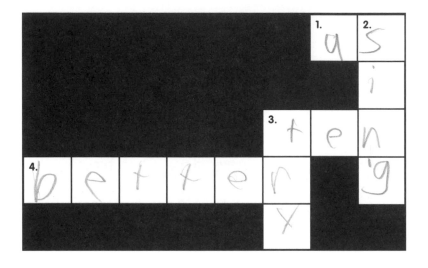

Across

1. Dad gave ___us___ a ride to school.

3. I have ___ten___ toes.

4. Yesterday I was sick, but today I feel ___better___.

Down

2. I can ___sing___ very loud.

3. Let's ___try___ our best to win the game.

Review: High Five

Look for the review words as you read the sentences inside each box. Put a check in the box that uses all five review words.

1. I was sick for ten days. I decided to sing a happy song. It made me feel better.

2. Mom told us to try a new food. It tasted better than I thought it would! I ate ten bites.

3. There are ten of us in the choir. We try to sing even better every day.

4. Our teacher helped us learn to sing better. We practice for ten minutes a day.

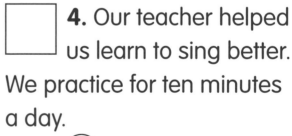

 **say the word wish aloud as you trace it.**

Now practice writing the word once on each line.

I _____ for a new doll.

Search and Splash

Find the word **wish** three times in the word search.

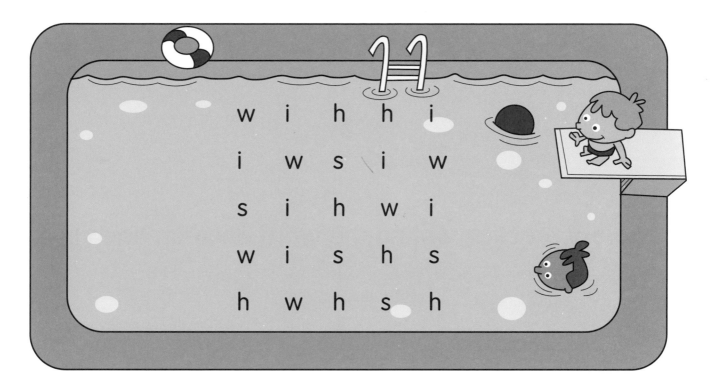

w i h h i
i w s i w
s i h w i
w i s h s
h w h s h

Do the letters go together to make the word **wish**?
Circle Yes or No.

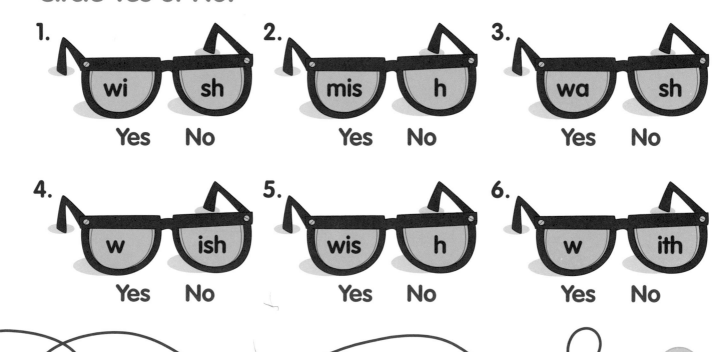

1. wi sh
   Yes   No

2. mis h
   Yes   No

3. wa sh
   Yes   No

4. w ish
   Yes   No

5. wis h
   Yes   No

6. w ith
   Yes   No

 **say the word fast aloud as you trace it.**

Now practice writing the word once on each line.

I can run _____!

What's the Order?

If the letters can be unscrambled to make the word fast, write it on the line. If the letters don't make the word fast, leave the line blank.

1. s a t f

_____

2. t s a t

_____

3. f t a c

_____

4. s f f a

_____

5. a f s t

_____

6. t f a s

_____

7. f i s t

_____

8. s t f s

_____

Unscramble the words to make a sentence. Write the sentence on the line.

meal   ate   You   fast.   your

_____

before *say the word* **before** *aloud as you trace it.*

before

Now practice writing the word once on each line.

You can go _____ me.

Stop and Go

Draw a line to connect the letters and make the word **before**.

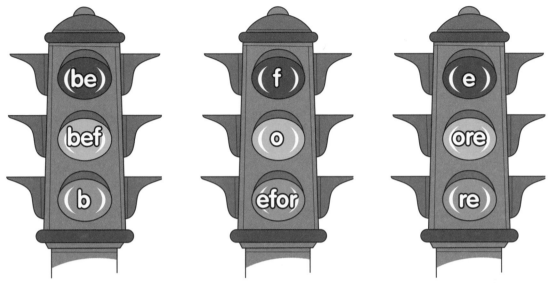

Fill in the blanks to complete the word **before**.

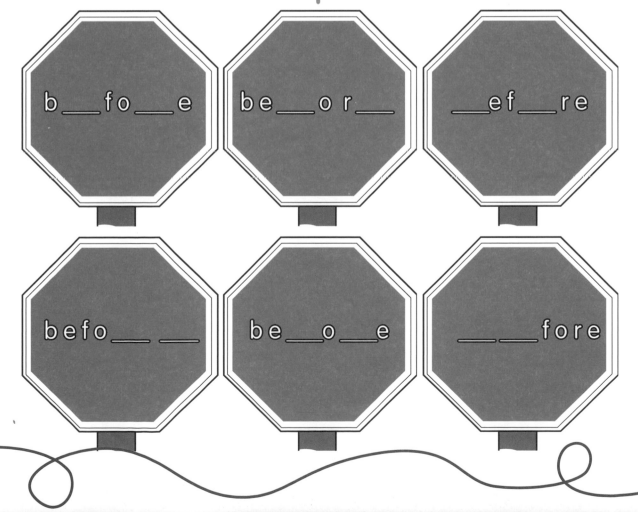

b__fo__e

be__or__

__ef__re

befo____

be__o__e

____fore

 **say the word fall aloud as you trace it.**

Now practice writing the word once on each line.

I always _____ down.

Amazing Maze

Look for the word **fall** in the maze. Connect all the words that spell **fall** to find your way out of the maze.

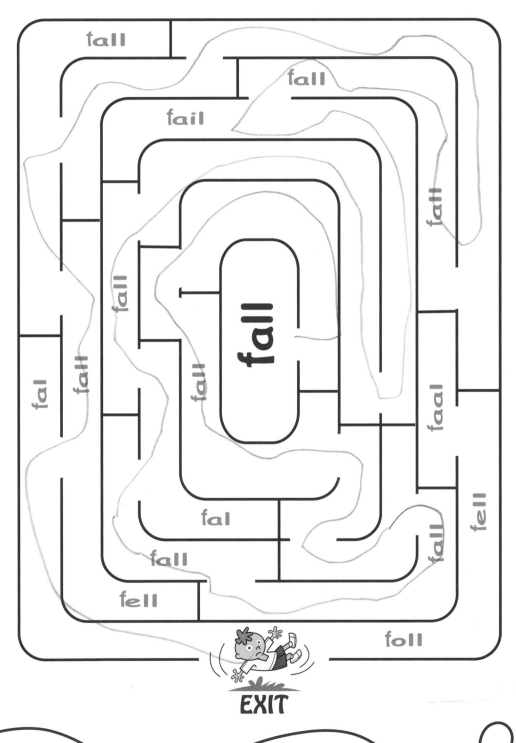

fall

fall

fail

fall

fall

fall

fal

fall

fall

fall

faal

fal

fell

fall

foll

fell

EXIT

 **say the word never aloud as you trace it.**

:::::: n̲e̲v̲e̲r̲ ::::::

Now practice writing the word once on each line.

You should _____ touch a hot stove.

Picture Puzzle

Find the word **never** in each sentence and circle it. Draw a line to connect the circled words in each sentence and see which letter your line passes through. Write the letters below to solve the picture puzzle.

1. I have never been to New York.

        l   d   b   g   n

2. I told my mom I would never do it again.

        w   e   r   a   i

3. I never wake up on time.

        c   a   b   o   m

4. The snow is something I have never seen.

        d   l   m   n   w

5. I would never tell a lie.

o L D

___ ___ ___ ___ ing old

Review: Crossword Puzzle!

Use the sentence clues below to solve the crossword puzzle.

wish   fast   before   fall   never

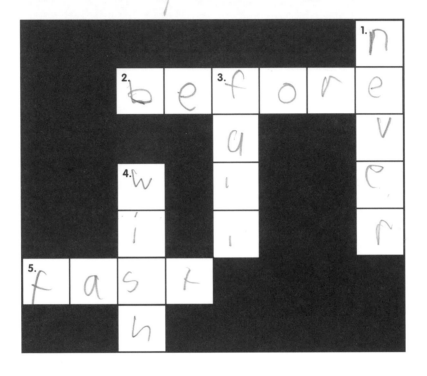

Across

2. Please wash your hands _____ dinner.

5. I can ride my bike _____ .

Down

1. You should _____ play with fire.

3. Don't _____ into that hole!

4. I _____ that I could fly.

Review: Story Code

Crack the code by writing the correct review word in each blank. Write the word that goes with each symbol in the box below.

My birthday _____ was to go to the lake. I had
            #

_____ been there _____. My _____ came true.
    *   &   #

_____ we left, my brother said, "Be careful not to _____
    &   @

in the lake!"

We got to the lake, and _____ anyone could stop me,
                                    &

I ran to the water very _____. I was running so _____ , I
                                !   !

fell into the water.

"I knew you would _____ in!" said my brother.
                            @

I _____ I had _____ gone to the lake!
    #   *

_____

* _____

& _____

@ _____

! _____

27

cut

Say the word cut aloud as you trace it.

Now practice writing the word once on each line.

I am getting my hair _____.

Keep on Track

Look for the word cut in each track. Circle it each time you see it. Then count the number of circled words in each track and write it in the sign.

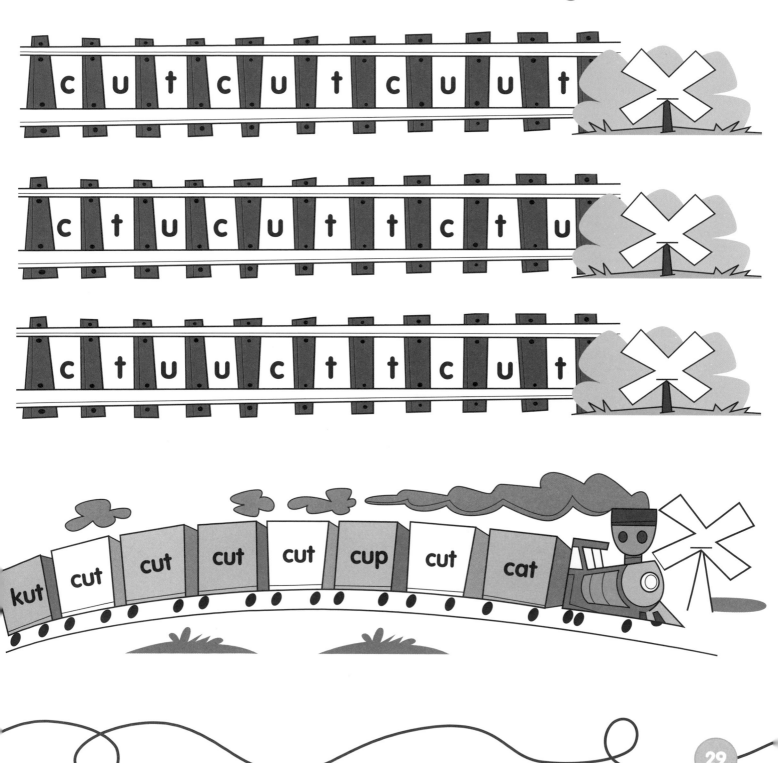

c u t c u t c u u t

c t u c u t t t c t u

c t u u c t t c u t

kut   cut   cut   cut   cut   cup   cut   cat

 **myself** *say the word* **myself** *aloud as you trace it.*

myself

Now practice writing the word once on each line.

I kept one cookie for _____.

Word Watch

Circle the birds that have the word **myself** inside.

 **say the word** hurt **aloud as you trace it.**

hurt

Now practice writing the word once on each line.

I _____ my knee.

Crack the Code

The word hurt is hidden once in each column. Find the word and circle the letters. Then use the code to complete the riddle below.

r	1: c	u	1: y	h	1: H
h	2: k	r	2: e	u	2: e
t	3: l	t	3: s	r	3: f
u	4: a	h	4: S	t	4: e
h	5: r	h	5: l	r	5: a
u	6: e	U	6: t	h	6: t
n	7: n	r	7: c	u	7: h
t	8: o	t	8: r	t	8: e
h	9: u	h	9: w	r	9: s
u	10: m	U	10: a	t	10: r
r	11: m	r	11: s	h	11: e
t	12: y	r	12: n	U	12: t

Why did the cookie go to the doctor?

__ __   __ __ __ __
1   2   3   4   5   6

__ __ __ __ __ __!
7   8   9   10   11   12

 **say the word far aloud as you trace it.**

Now practice writing the word once on each line.

How _____ away is the beach?

Target Words

Circle the words that have **far** hidden inside.
Underline the letters **f-a-r** in each circled word.

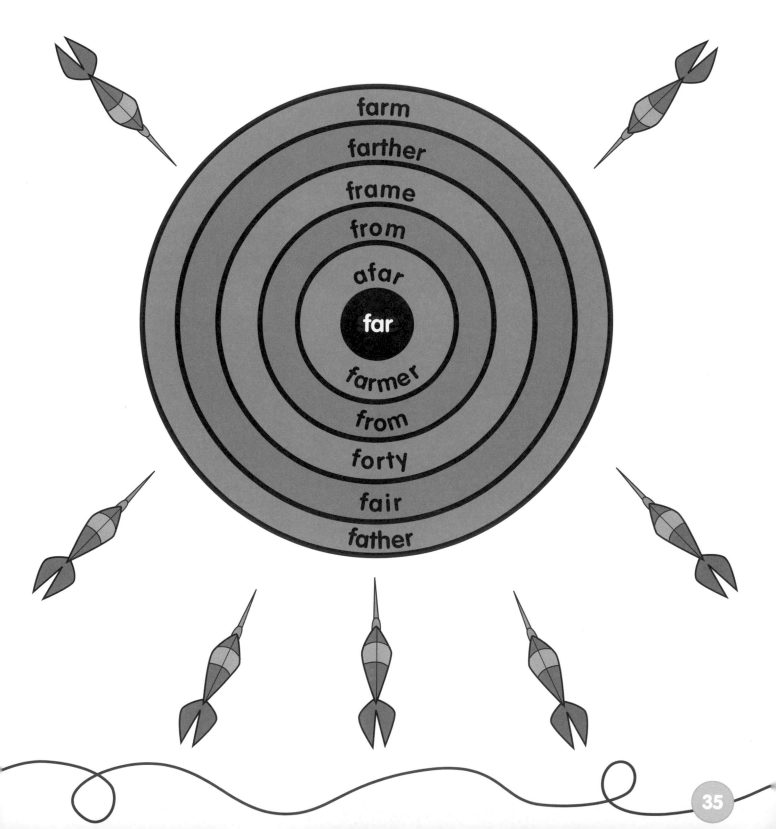

farm
farther
frame
from
afar
far
farmer
from
forty
fair
father

because

say the word because aloud as you trace it.

because

Now practice writing the word once on each line.

A vase broke _____ I dropped it.

Pen Pals

Circle the word **because** every time it appears in the letters. Count how many circled words are in each letter, and write the number in the box. Find out which pen pal used the word **because** more.

Dear Emily,

I can't go to the beach today because it's raining. Rainy days are nice because I can stay inside and write letters. I am excited because I can use my new pen. My dad gave it to me because I did well on my spelling test. I hope to become the best speller in my class! I study every night because I want to be in the spelling bee!

Sincerely,

Anna

Dear Anna,

I like getting your letters because they are always fun to read. I like rainy days too, but not because I can write letters. I like rainy days because I can read by the fire. Sometimes on rainy days I read old letters from my pen pals. I never throw away a letter because I might want to read it again. I keep all my letters in a box right beside my bed.

Sincerely,

Emily

Review: Crossword Puzzle!

Use the sentence clues below to solve the crossword puzzle.

cut   myself   hurt   far   because

Across

2. I'm sleepy _____ it's very late.

4. When I fell off my bike, I _____ my foot.

5. My grandma lives very _____ away.

Down

1. I did the dishes all by _____ .

3. Please _____ the paper into two pieces.

Review: High Five

Look for the review words as you read the sentences inside each box. Put a check in the box that uses all five review words.

1. I cut my sandwich in half because my friend had no lunch. I gave half to him and ate the other half myself.

2. We take the bus to school because it's too far to walk. I read quietly to myself while I'm on the bus.

3. I need to see the nurse because I hurt myself. I cut my hand playing outside.

4. I stepped on some glass and cut myself. I couldn't walk very far because my foot hurt.

clean

say the word clean aloud as you trace it.

clean

Now practice writing the word once on each line.

I need to put on some _____ clothes.

Search and Splash

Find the word **clean** three times in the word search.

```
c   n   c   l   e
e   l   l   e   n
c   l   e   a   n
l   a   a   a   c
e   n   n   l   n
```

Do the letters go together to make the word **clean**?
Circle Yes or No.

1. cle   an
   Yes   No

2. cle   en
   Yes   No

3. cl   aen
   Yes   No

4. c   leen
   Yes   No

5. cl   ean
   Yes   No

6. clea   n
   Yes   No

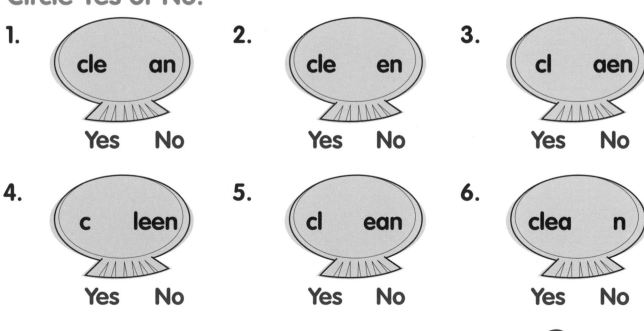

much

Say the word much aloud as you trace it.

much

Now practice writing the word once on each line.

How ______________ does it cost?

What's the Order?

If the letters can be unscrambled to make the word much, write it on the line. If the letters don't make the word much, leave the line blank.

1. c h m a

_____

2. m u c k

_____

3. u h m c

_____

4. m h c u

_____

5. c u m h

_____

6. c h n u

_____

7. h m u c

_____

8. c n m u

_____

Unscramble the words to make a sentence. Write the sentence on the line.

do   much   you   How   want?

_____

 **would** *say the word* **would** *aloud as you trace it.*

would

Now practice writing the word once on each line.

What flavor _____ you like?

Stop and Go

Draw a line to connect the letters and make the word **would**.

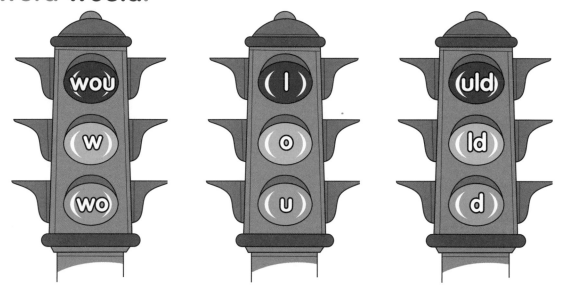

Fill in the blanks to complete the word **would**.

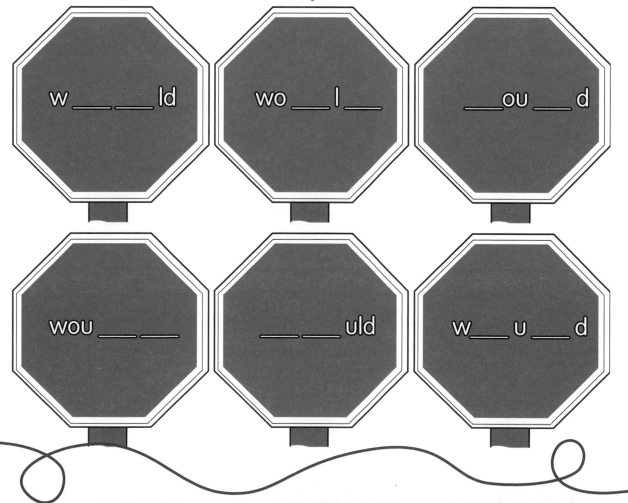

w __ __ ld

wo __ l __

__ ou __ d

wou __ __

__ __ uld

w __ u __ d

 **say the word kind aloud as you trace it.**

Now practice writing the word once on each line.

I try to be _____ to others.

Amazing Maze

Look for the word **kind** in the maze. Connect all the words that spell **kind** to find your way out of the maze.

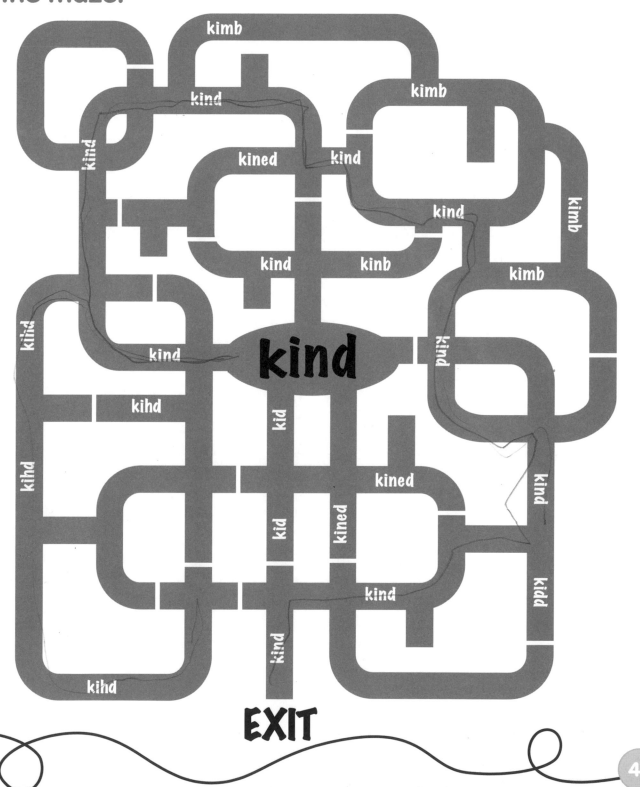

EXIT

 **carry** say the word carry aloud as you trace it.

carry

Now practice writing the word once on each line.

I can _____ my baby sister.

Picture Puzzle

Find the word **carry** in each sentence and circle it. Draw a line to connect the circled words in each sentence and see which letter your line passes through. Write the letters below to solve the picture puzzle.

1. Please carry your plate to the sink.

      l   a   s   t   i

2. My bag is too heavy to carry.

      w   g   y   a   i

3. I like to carry my brother on my back.

      c   g   y   i   l

4. There are too many books to carry.

      d   e   p   l   w

5. I can't carry this to the car!

T
A
L
E   _____ _____ _____ _____ tale

Review: Crossword Puzzle!

Use the sentence clues below to solve the crossword puzzles.

clean   much   carry   kind   would

Across

3. Can you _____ the box outside?

5. What _____ you like to watch on TV?

Down

1. We need to _____ up our room.

2. It was _____ of you to help me.

4. I have too _____ work to do!

Review: Story Code

Crack the code by writing the correct review word in each blank. Write the word that goes with each symbol in the box below.

I have a very _____ neighbor. She always helps us
_#

_____ the groceries in from the car. My family likes
_!

her very _____ .
_@

One day, she asked if I _____ help her. She needed to
_*

_____ out her garage. There was too _____ stuff for
_&   _@

her to _____ . I told her I _____ help her.
_!   _*

When we were done, her garage was so _____ ! It felt
_&

good to do something _____ for her.
_#

```
# _____
* _____
& _____
@ _____
! _____
```

 **six** say the word **six**
aloud as you trace it.

_____

:::::: six _____

Now practice writing the word once on each line.

_____

....

_____

_____

....

_____

_____

....

_____

....

_____

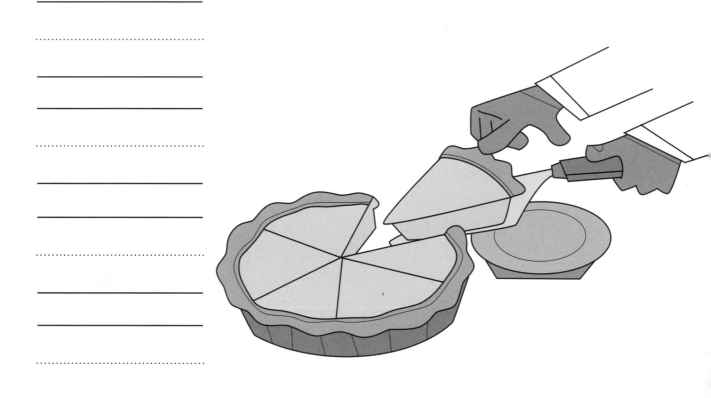

There are _____ slices of pie.

Keep Track

Look for the word **six** in each track. Circle it each time you see it. Then count the number of circled words in each track and write it in the sign.

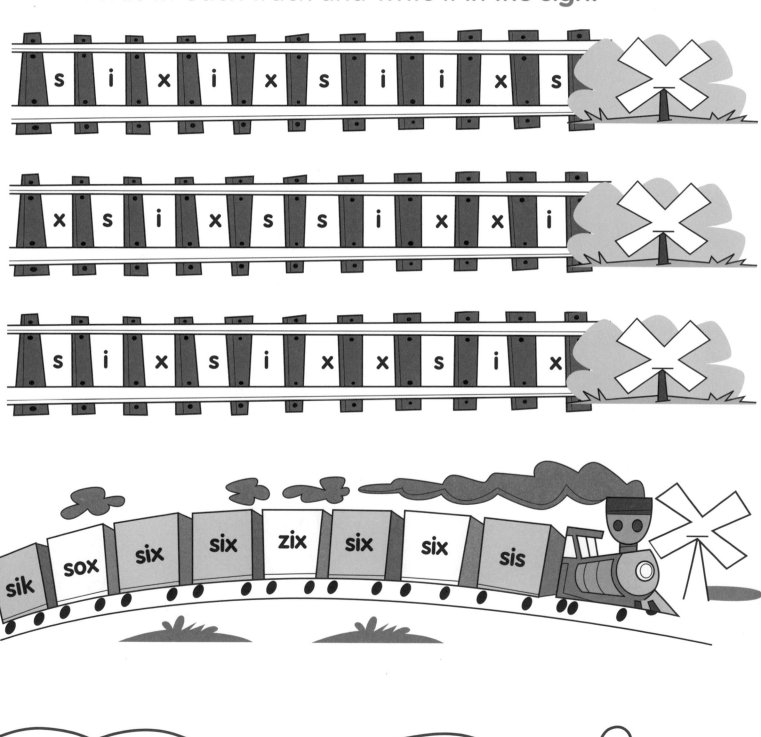

 **show** say the word show aloud as you trace it.

Now practice writing the word once on each line.

Let me _____ **you my picture.**

Word Watch

Circle the birds that have the word show inside.

shoe

shaw

show

show

show

show

shov

zhow

shoow

show

done

say the word done aloud as you trace it.

done

Now practice writing the word once on each line.

I am all _____ eating.

Crack the Code

The word **done** is hidden once in each column. Find the word and circle the letters. Then use the code to complete the riddle below.

d	1: F	d	1: c	o	1: V
o	2: i	o	2: o	d	2: e
n	3: r	n	3: d	n	3: r
e	4: e	n	4: e	e	4: y
d	5: a	d	5: g	d	5: c
o	6: t	o	6: A	o	6: r
e	7: h	e	7: t	n	7: a
n	8: i	n	8: h	e	8: c
e	9: t	d	9: k	n	9: l
d	10: r	o	10: e	o	10: a
o	11: u	n	11: r	d	11: r
n	12: n	e	12: s	e	12: b

What do firemen put in their soup?

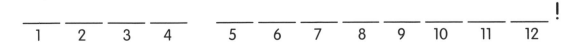

___ ___ ___ ___ ___ ___ ___ ___ ___ ___ ___ ___ !
 1   2   3   4   5   6   7   8   9   10   11   12

long

say the word long aloud as you trace it.

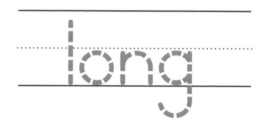

Now practice writing the word once on each line.

My hair is very _____.

Target Words

Circle the words that have **long** hidden inside.
Underline the letters l-o-n-g in each circled word.

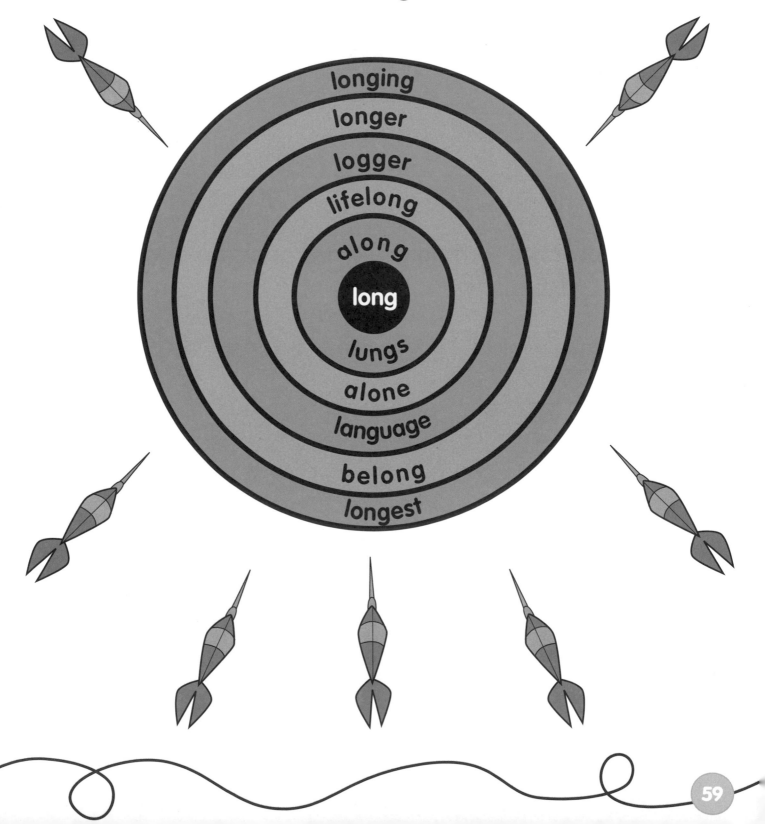

longing
longer
logger
lifelong
along
long
lungs
alone
language
belong
longest

always say the word always aloud as you trace it.

always

Now practice writing the word once on each line.

I _____ do my chores.

Pen Pals

Circle the word **always** every time it appears in the letters. Count how many circled words are in each letter, and write the number in the box. Find out which pen pal used the word **always** more.

Dear Noah,

Whenever I go on a trip, I always bring a pen and paper along. It's always fun to send you a letter about my trip. My family always camps at the same place every year. This year, the place we always go to is full. So we drove around until we found a new place to camp. I like the new place even better!

Sincerely,

Gabe

Dear Gabe,

I always like reading your letters. You always have a fun story to tell. My family always camps at the same place too. Whenever we camp, we always go on a hike. I wanted to go on the hike alone, but my parents wouldn't allow it. They said you should always hike with a buddy.

Sincerely,

Noah

Review: Crossword Puzzle!

Use the sentence clues below to solve the crossword puzzle.

six   show   done   long   always

Across

3. There is a _____ line for the restroom.

4. Will you _____ me your new dress?

5. We eat dinner at _____ o'clock.

Down

1. Put the game away when you're _____ playing.

2. I _____ wear a helmet when I ride my bike.

Review: High Five

Look for the review words as you read the sentences inside each box. Put a check in the box that uses all five review words.

1. We always have dinner at six o'clock. When we're done, we take a long walk.

2. I always show my paintings to my mom. I've done this since I was six years old.

3. When I'm done surfing, I always show people that my board is six feet long.

4. How long will it be until the pie is done? I always show it to the family before we eat it.

Say the word shall aloud as you trace it.

shall

Now practice writing the word once on each line.

When _____ we have dinner?

Search and Splash

Find the word shall three times in the word search.

s s h a l

s h a l l

h a a a s

a l h l h

l l s l l

Do the letters go together to make the word shall? Circle Yes or No.

1.

sha al

Yes   No

2.

sh ale

Yes   No

3.

shal ll

Yes   No

4.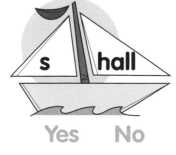

s hall

Yes   No

5.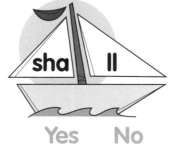

sha ll

Yes   No

6.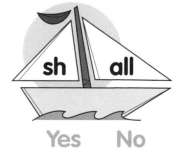

sh all

Yes   No

 **which** *say the word* **which** *aloud as you trace it.*

which

Now practice writing the word once on each line.

_____ hat should I wear?

What's the Order?

If the letters can be unscrambled to make the word **which**, write it on the line. If the letters don't make the word **which**, leave the line blank.

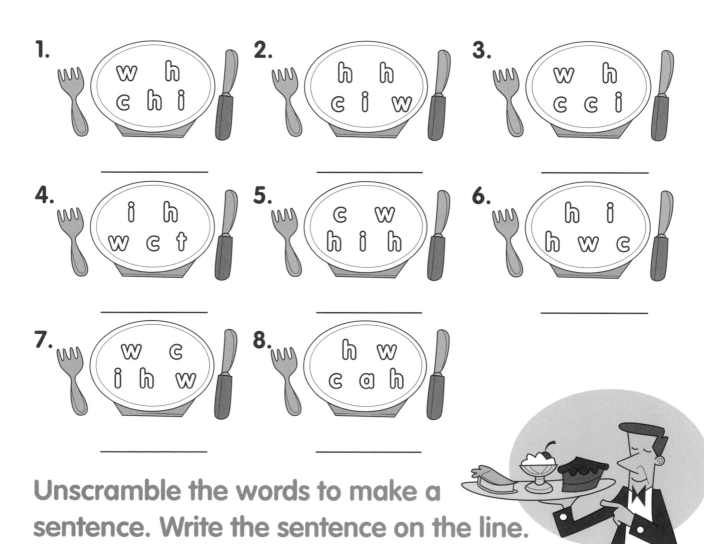

1. w h c h i
_____

2. h h c i w
_____

3. w h c c i
_____

4. i h w c t
_____

5. c w h i h
_____

6. h i h w c
_____

7. w c i h w
_____

8. h w c a h
_____

Unscramble the words to make a sentence. Write the sentence on the line.

want   one   Which   you   do?

_____

 **bring**

say the word bring aloud as you trace it.

bring

Now practice writing the word once on each line.

You should _____ **a warm coat.**

Stop and Go

Draw a line to connect the letters and make the word bring.

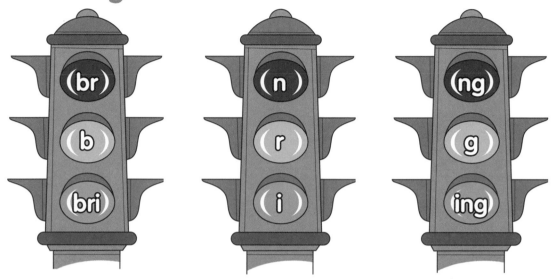

Fill in the blanks to complete the word bring.

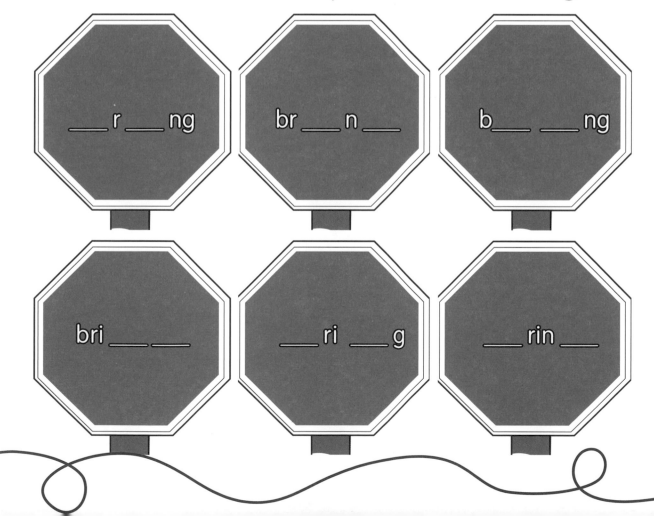

__ r __ ng

br __ n __

b__ __ ng

bri __ __

__ ri __ g

__ rin __

 **say the word only aloud as you trace it.**

Now practice writing the word once on each line.

There is _____ one apple left.

Amazing Maze

Look for the word **only** in the maze. Connect all the words that spell **only** to find your way out of the maze.

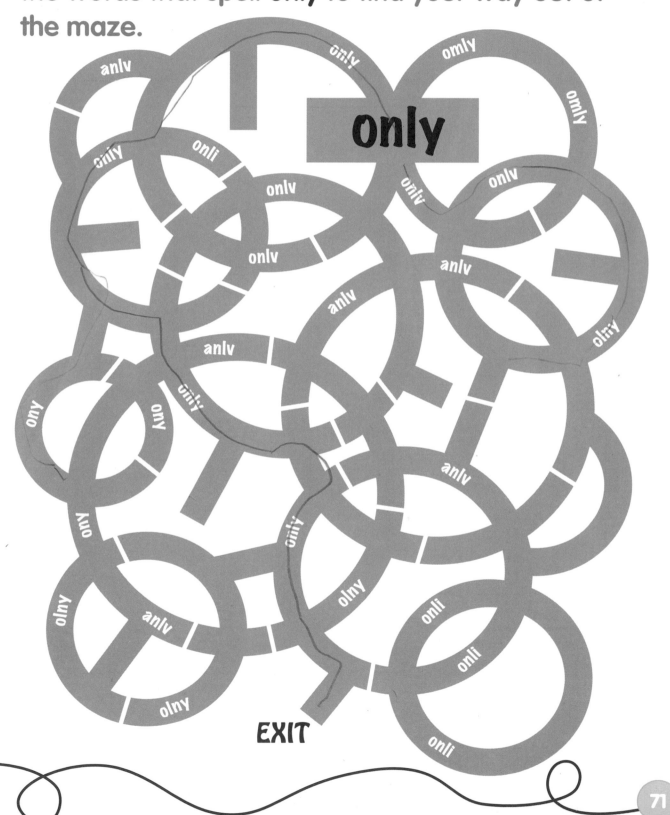

EXIT

 **small**

say the word small aloud as you trace it.

small

Now practice writing the word once on each line.

A mouse is very _____.

Picture Puzzle

Find the word **small** in each sentence and circle it. Draw a line to connect the circled words in each sentence and see which letter your line passes through. Write the letters below to solve the picture puzzle.

1. This shirt is too small.

s   i   f   g   r

2. A small bug was on the ground.

o   e   a   t   b

3. I would like to order a small drink.

c   o   v   l   y

4. I'm too small to go on that ride.

h   t   w   l   s

5. These shoes are too small.

S

   T

      A

         R   ___ ___ ___ ___ ing star

Review: Crossword Puzzle!

Use the sentence clues below to solve the crossword puzzle.

shall   which   small   only   bring

Across

2. You need to

_____ the box over here.

3. What _____ we do today?

4. I am the _____ one who hit a home run.

Down

1. _____ way should we go?

3. I would like a _____ bowl of soup.

Review: Story Code

Crack the code by writing the correct review word in each blank. Write the word that goes with each symbol in the box below.

What _____ we do when Grandpa comes to visit? He

#

will _____ be here for a few days. I told him to _____

@   *

his favorite game. I wonder _____ game he will _____.

&   *

_____ room will Grandpa sleep in? My room is,

&

very _____ and I _____ have one pillow. Grandpa says

!   @

that my room is not too _____ for him. He will _____ his

!   *

own pillow. So, we _____ be roommates!

#

_____

* _____

& _____

@ _____

! _____

Review: ABC Gumballs

Write the review words in alphabetical order.

1. _____ 2. _____ 3. _____

4. _____ 5. _____ 6. _____

7. _____ 8. _____ 9. _____

10. _____ 11. _____ 12. _____

13. _____ 14. _____ 15. _____

Review: Sentence Squares

Read each group of sentences. Then find the group of words below that completes the sentences. Fill the missing words in the blanks.

1. When Grandma comes to visit _____ , she likes to _____ gifts. She has _____ this for a _____ time, and we like it very _____.

2. My sister _____ does _____ things. When I _____ my foot, she helped _____ me home. I will _____ to be kind to her, too.

3. I needed to _____ my room _____ I made a mess. My room looked so much _____ , so I wanted to _____ it to my family. I was very proud of _____.

because   clean   myself
better   show

carry   kind   always
try   hurt

bring   long   us
much   done

 **say the word** hot **aloud as you trace it.**

hot

Now practice writing the word once on each line.

The water is too _____!

Keep on Track

Look for the word hot in each track. Circle it each time you see it. Then count the number of circled words in each track and write it in the sign.

| h | o | t | h | o | o | t | h | o | t |

| h | t | o | h | o | t | o | t | h | o |

| h | t | h | o | t | h | o | t | h | o |

hof hit hot not hot hot hut hat

 **drink**

say the word drink aloud as you trace it.

drink

Now practice writing the word once on each line.

I like to _____ milk.

Word Watch

Circle the birds that have the word **drink** inside.

their say the word their **aloud as you trace it.**

their

Now practice writing the word once on each line.

The boys are walking _____ dogs.

Crack the Code

The word their is hidden once in each column. Find the word and circle the letters. Then use the code to complete the riddle below.

t	**1: F**	t	**1: g**	t	**1: W**
h	**2: o**	h	**2: r**	h	**2: i**
e	**3: r**	e	**3: l**	e	**3: t**
r	**4: t**	r	**4: b**	i	**4: h**
e	**5: h**	e	**5: n**	r	**5: t**
t	**6: o**	t	**6: t**	h	**6: e**
h	**7: m**	h	**7: k**	t	**7: r**
e	**8: a**	r	**8: o**	e	**8: s**
i	**9: t**	e	**9: a**	i	**9: l**
r	**10: o**	i	**10: d**	r	**10: a**
t	**11: a**	t	**11: p**	t	**11: r**
h	**12: n**	h	**12: a**	h	**12: b**
i	**13: d**	e	**13: s**	e	**13: r**
e	**14: g**	i	**14: t**	i	**14: a**
r	**15: o**	r	**15: e**	e	**15: d**

How do you repair a broken tomato?

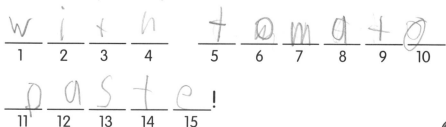

w i t h   t o m a t o
1   2   3   4   5   6   7   8   9   10

p a s t e !
11   12   13   14   15

GLUE

say the word light aloud as you trace it.

light

Now practice writing the word once on each line.

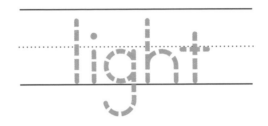

Turn on the _____.

Target Words

Circle the words that have **light** hidden inside.
Underline the letters **l-i-g-h-t** in each circled word.

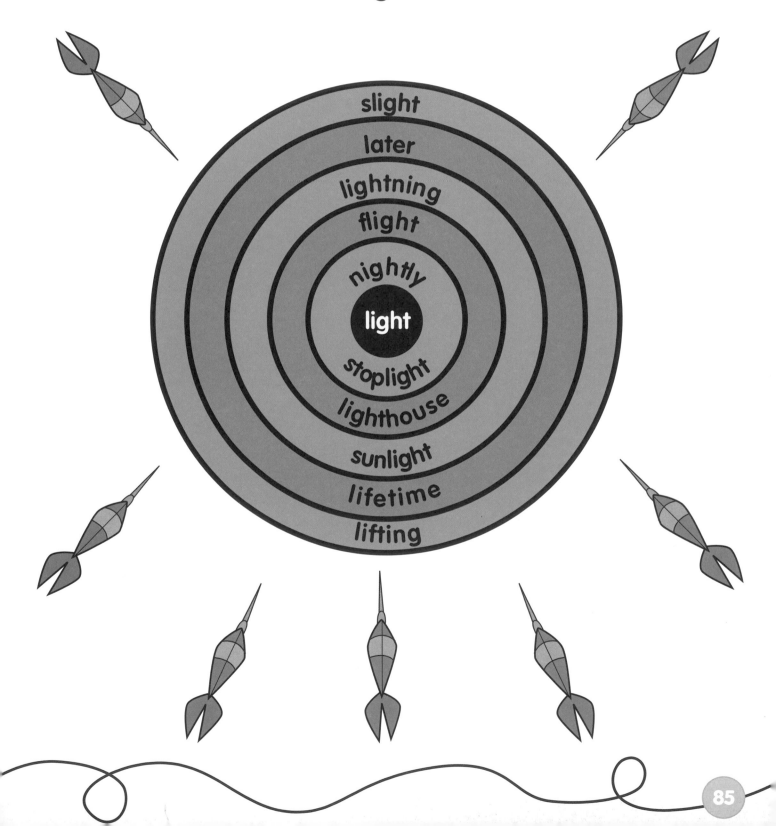

slight
later
lightning
flight
nightly
light
stoplight
lighthouse
sunlight
lifetime
lifting

 **if**

Say the word if aloud as you trace it.

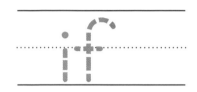

Now practice writing the word once on each line.

We'll go to the beach
_____ it's sunny.

Pen Pals

Circle the word **if** every time it appears in the letters. Count how many circled words are in each letter, and write the number in the box. Find out which pen pal used the word **if** more.

Dear Bonnie,

I wonder if we can see each other this summer. Do you know if you are taking a summer vacation? It would be fun to see you if you are in my area. I will ask my parents if you can stay with us. If you want, we can sleep in a tent in my backyard.

Sincerely,

Betty

Dear Betty,

I will ask my parents if I can come to visit you. I'm sure that if we are in your area, it will be okay. It would be fun to sleep in a tent if it's not too cold. I've always wanted to do that! If we talk to our parents about it, I bet they will say yes!

Sincerely,

Bonnie

Review: Crossword Puzzle!

Use the sentence clues below to solve the crossword puzzle.

hot   drink   their   light   if

Across

2. It's dark in here! Who turned off the _____ ?

4. We go swimming when it's _____ outside.

5. Ask your mom _____ you can play.

Down

1. I need to get a _____ of water.

3. My brothers have a bunk bed in _____ room.

Review: High Five

Look for the review words as you read the sentences inside each box. Put a check in the box that uses all five review words.

1. ☐ If I wake up before it's light outside, I make hot chocolate for my family. It's their favorite drink.

2. ☐ My brothers forgot to turn off their bedroom light. The lightbulb gets very hot if it's on all day long.

3. ☐ My parents like to drink hot tea every night. Then they turn out the light and go to sleep.

4. ☐ If I can't fall asleep, I turn on the light and get a drink of hot milk.

say the word draw aloud as you trace it.

Now practice writing the word once on each line.

I like to _____ pictures.

Search and Splash

Find the word **draw** three times in the word search.

d	r	w	w	d
r	d	a	d	r
a	r	d	r	a
d	a	r	a	a
w	w	a	w	w

Do the letters go together to make the word **draw**?
Circle Yes or No.

1.  **dra   w**   Yes   No

2.  **dr   raw**   Yes   No

3.  **br   aw**   Yes   No

4.  **dr   aw**   Yes   No

5.  **dra   v v**   Yes   No

6.  **d   raw**   Yes   No

 **seven**

say the word seven aloud as you trace it.

seven

Now practice writing the word once on each line.

There are _____ days in a week.

What's the Order?

If the letters can be unscrambled to make the word seven, write it on the line. If the letters don't make the word seven, leave the line blank.

1. v s e n v

_____

2. s e n e w

_____

3. v e s n e

_____

4. e e s v n

_____

5. s n e e v

_____

6. v e s e m

_____

7. s e v e r

_____

8. v s n e e

_____

Unscramble the words to make a sentence. Write the sentence on the line.

pie.   of   are   There   seven   slices

_____

Say the word write aloud as you trace it.

write

Now practice writing the word once on each line.

I can _____ my name on the board.

Stop and Go

Draw a line to connect the letters and make the word **write**.

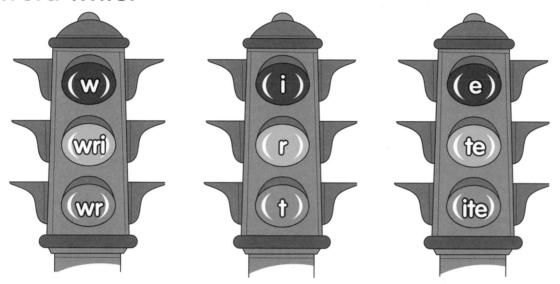

Fill in the blanks to complete the word **write**.

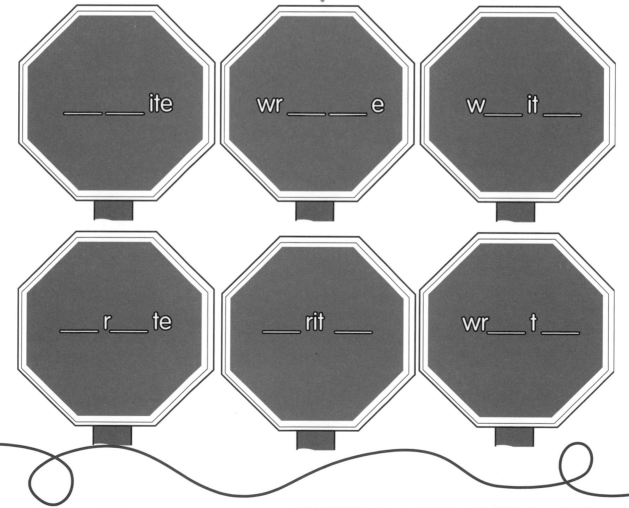

____ ____ ite

wr ____ ____ e

w __ it ____

__ r __ te

__ rit ____

wr __ t ____

 **around**

Say the word around aloud as you trace it.

around

Now practice writing the word once on each line.

The puppy runs _____ the tree.

Amazing Maze

Look for the word around in the maze. Connect all the words that spell around to find your way out of the maze.

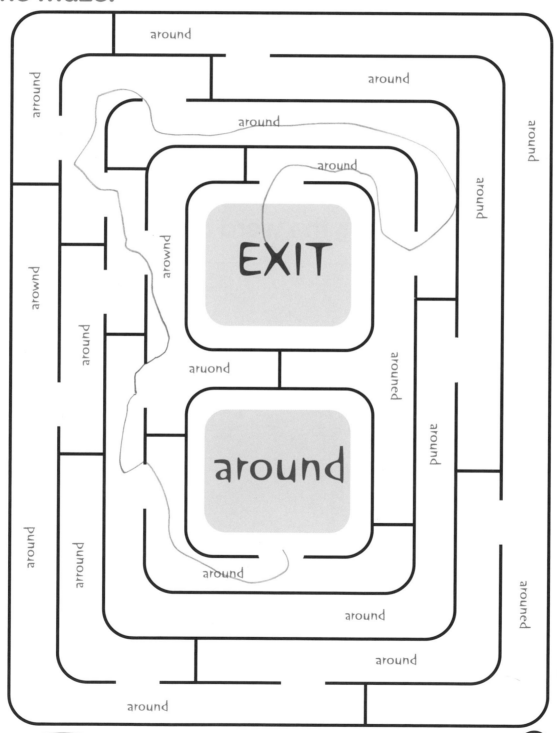

 **say the word about aloud as you trace it.**

about

Now practice writing the word once on each line.

This book is all _____ bees.

Picture Puzzle

Find the word **about** in each sentence and circle it. Draw a line to connect the circled words in each sentence and see which letter your line passes through. Write the letters below to solve the picture puzzle.

1. Tell me all about yourself.

       l   c   d   r   s

2. I don't know what that movie is about.

       n   a   g   i   q

3. Talk about your summer plans.

       c   a   b   u   m

4. I need to write a report about robots.

       d   c   d   e   a

5. We learned about animals at the zoo.

```
                    dance
          d                   d
          a                   a
          n                   n
          c                   c
          e                   e
                    dance

          ____ ____ ____ ____ re   dance
```

Review: Crossword Puzzle!

Use the sentence clues below to solve the crossword puzzle.

draw   seven   write   around   about

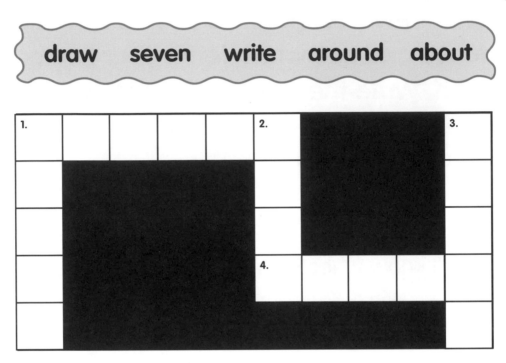

Across

1. Put a circle _____ the answer.

4. I like to _____ letters to my friends.

Down

1. I wrote a story _____ my dog.

2. In art class we _____ pictures.

3. My sister is _____ years old.

Review: Story Code

Crack the code by writing the correct review word in each blank. Write the word that goes with each symbol in the box below.

When I was _____ years old, we moved to a new
              @

town. I was sad _____ moving. My friends gathered
                 #

_____ to say goodbye. We said we would _____
 *   &

letters.

Our new house was so big, it had _____ bedrooms.
                                    @

We had a big yard where our dog could run _____ . I didn't
                                             *

forget to _____ my friends and tell them _____ our
            &   #

newhouse. They wrote back and asked me to _____ a
                                              !

picture of my new house. It was fun to _____ pictures and
                                          !

_____ my friends letters.
 &

```
#  _____
*  _____
&  _____
@  _____
!  _____
```

MOVING

 **say the word got aloud as you trace it.**

Now practice writing the word once on each line.

I _____ a puppy for my birthday.

Keep on Track

Look for the word **got** in each track. Circle it each time you see it. Then count the number of circled words in each track and write it in the sign.

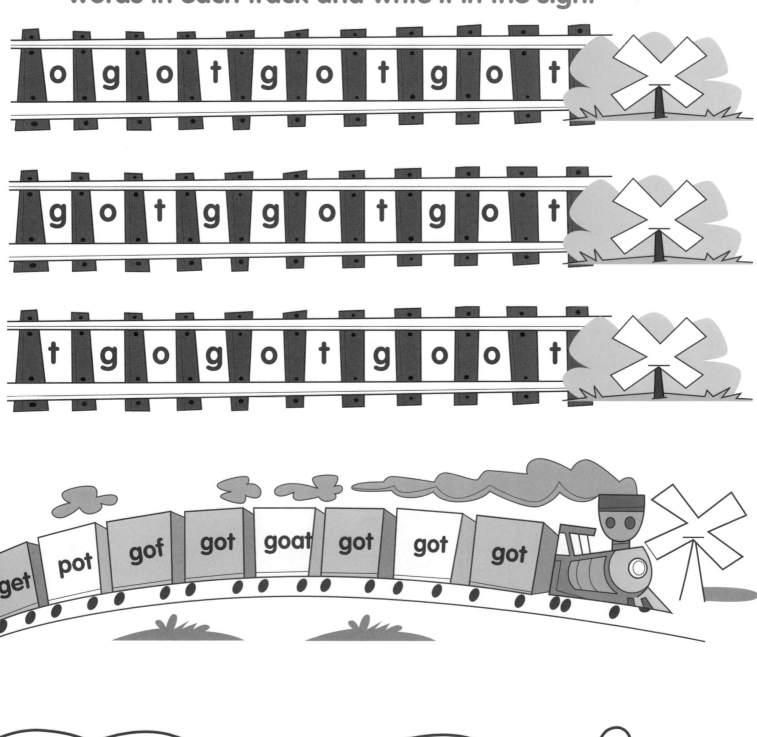

o g o t g o t g o t g o t

g o t g g o t g o t

t g o g o t g o t g o o t

get pot gof got goat got got got

say the word keep aloud as you trace it.

keep

Now practice writing the word once on each line.

You can _____ your toys in the box.

Word Watch

Circle the birds that have the word keep inside.

 **say the word both aloud as you trace it.**

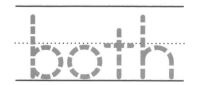

Now practice writing the word once on each line.

We _____ have the same hat.

Crack the Code

The word **both** is hidden once in each column. Find the word and circle the letters. Then use the code to complete the riddle below.

b	**1: a**	b	**1: A**	b	**1: d**
o	**2: g**	o	**2: j**	a	**2: o**
o	**3: i**	t	**3: e**	t	**3: n**
t	**4: f**	h	**4: l**	h	**4: v**
h	**5: W**	b	**5: p**	b	**5: l**
b	**6: a**	o	**6: r**	o	**6: y**
o	**7: y**	h	**7: i**	t	**7: b**
t	**8: l**	t	**8: t**	h	**8: u**
b	**9: t**	d	**9: y**	o	**9: T**
o	**10: t**	o	**10: e**	t	**10: h**
t	**11: o**	t	**11: d**	h	**11: i**
h	**12: n**	h	**12: s**	b	**12: r**

What's in the middle of a jellyfish?

_A_ _j_ _e_ _l_ _l_ _y_
 1   2   3   4   5   6

_b_ _y_ _t_ _t_ _o_ _n_ !
 7   8   9 10 11 12

 **grow**

say the word grow aloud as you trace it.

Now practice writing the word once on each line.

Plants need the sun to _____.

Target Words

Circle the words that have **grow** hidden inside.
Underline the letters **g-r-o-w** in each circled word.

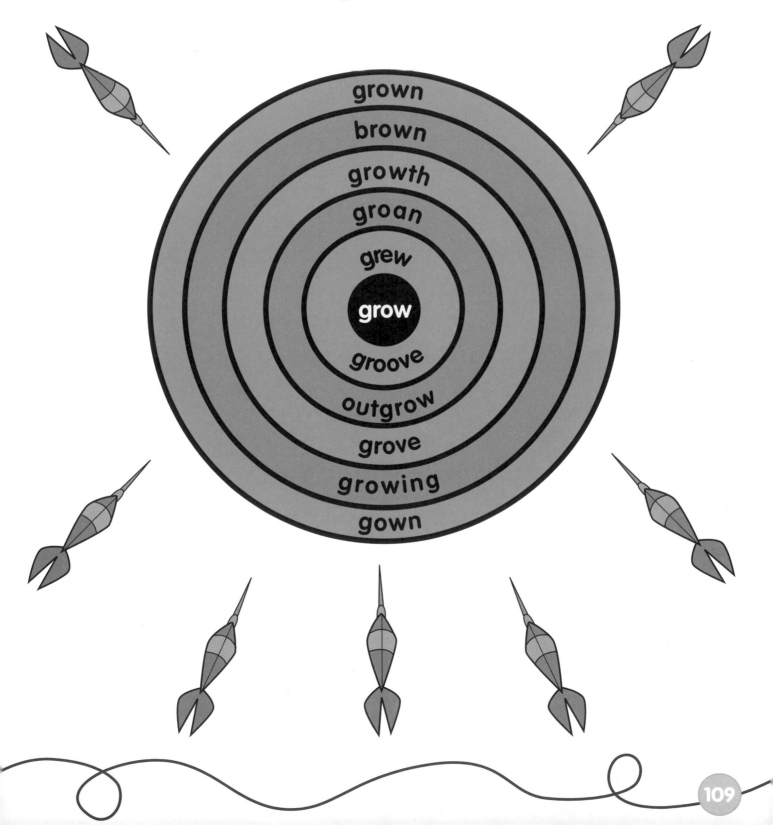

grown
brown
growth
groan
grew
grow
groove
outgrow
grove
growing
gown

 **together** *say the word together aloud as you trace it.*

togetheer

Now practice writing the word once on each line.

Let's walk home _____.

Pen Pals

Circle the word together every time it appears in the letters. Count how many circled words are in each letter, and write the number in the box. Find out which pen pal used the word together more.

Dear Jake,

I can't wait to get together this weekend. I've planned lots of fun things for us to do together. We can play in the backyard together. I like to gather up all the leaves and make a big pile. Together, we can make the biggest pile ever! See you soon!

Sincerely,

Steve

Dear Steve,

We always have fun when we're together. My dad and I will ride together on the train to get to your house. We will play games together to pass the time. I'll bring my basketball with me. Maybe we can get together a group to play basketball. I'm excited to spend time together.

Sincerely,

Jake

Review: Crossword Puzzle!

Use the sentence clues below to solve the crossword puzzle.

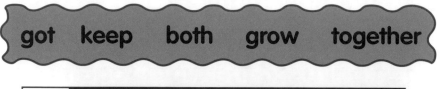

got   keep   both   grow   together

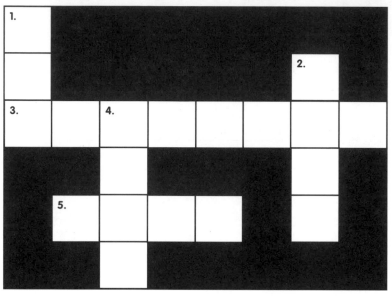

Across

3. Let's go to the party _____ .

5. The present is for _____ of us.

Down

1. I _____ some new shoes for school.

2. Please _____ this door open.

4. When I _____ up, I want to be a teacher.

Review: High Five

Look for the review words as you read the sentences inside each box. Put a check in the box that uses all five review words.

☐ **1.** I keep both of my fish together in the same tank. I got some new fish food to help them grow.

☐ **2.** My sister and I both like to grow flowers together. We keep all of our gardening tools in the yard.

☐ **3.** My friend got two puppies this year. He takes both of them on walks together. They are starting to grow into big dogs.

☐ **4.** Dad got a gift for both me and my brother. We opened it together. We plan to keep it forever.

 **say the word pick aloud as you trace it.**

pick

Now practice writing the word once on each line.

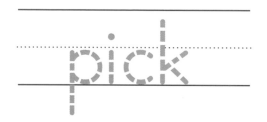

You can _____ a book to read.

Search and Splash

Find the word **pick** three times in the word search.

p i c p k

p p k i c

i p i c k

c i c k p

k c k p i

Do the letters go together to make the word **pick**?
Circle Yes or No.

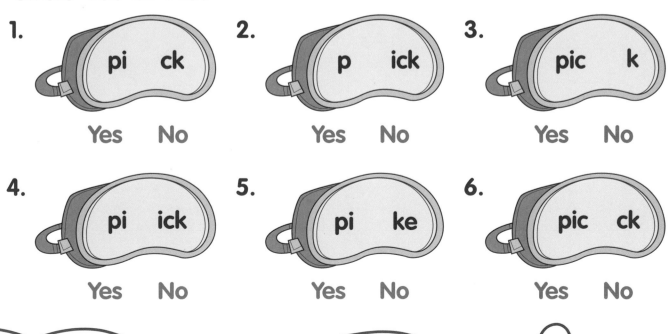

1. pi ck

Yes   No

2. p ick

Yes   No

3. pic k

Yes   No

4. pi ick

Yes   No

5. pi ke

Yes   No

6. pic ck

Yes   No

Say the word eight aloud as you trace it.

Now practice writing the word once on each line.

A spider has _____ legs.

What's the Order?

If the letters can be unscrambled to make the word **eight**, write it on the line. If the letters don't make the word **eight**, leave the line blank.

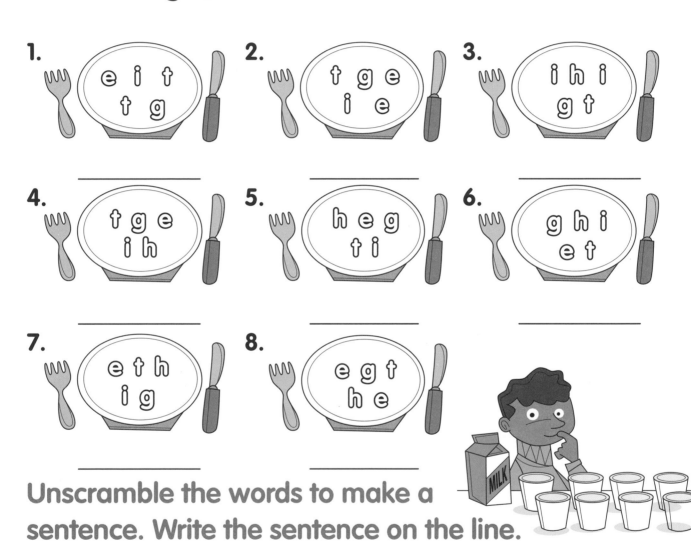

1. e i t t g
_____

2. t g e i e
_____

3. i h i g t
_____

4. t g e i h
_____

5. h e g t i
_____

6. g h i e t
_____

7. e t h i g
_____

8. e g t h e
_____

Unscramble the words to make a sentence. Write the sentence on the line.

glasses   milk.   I   of   drank   eight

_____

 **today**

say the word today **aloud as** *you trace it.*

today

Now practice writing the word once on each line.

We're going to the zoo _____.

Stop and Go

Draw a line to connect the letters and make the word **today**.

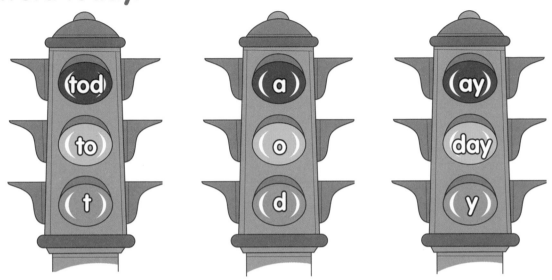

Fill in the blanks to complete the word **today**.

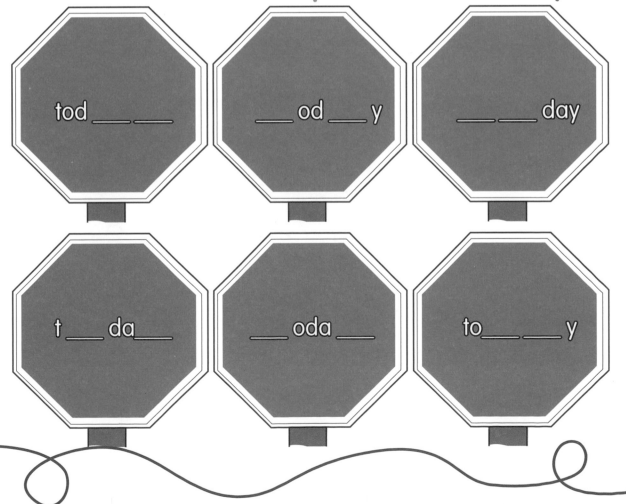

tod _____ _____

_____ od _____ y

_____ _____ _____ day

t _____ da _____

_____ oda _____

to _____ _____ y

**work**

Now practice writing the word once on each line.

My mom goes to _____ every day.

Amazing Maze

Look for the word work in the maze. Connect all the words that spell work to find your way out of the maze.

Say the word start aloud as you trace it.

start

Now practice writing the word once on each line.

It's time to _____ the race.

Picture Puzzle

Find the word **start** in each sentence and circle it. Draw a line to connect the circled words in each sentence and see which letter your line passes through. Write the letters below to solve the picture puzzle.

1. Don't start the game without me.

      l   t   o   h   g

2. When does the movie start?

      w   y   l   a   i

3. Wash your hands before you start.

      c   r   w   g   c

4. Start the timer now, please.

      p   h   r   s   n

5. You can start first, and I'll go next.

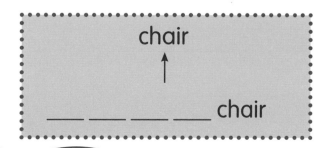

chair

____ ____ ____ ____ chair

Review: Crossword Puzzle!

Use the sentence clues below to solve the crossword puzzle.

pick   eight   today   work   start

Across

2. What do you want to do _____ ?

4. The trip will take _____ hours.

5. After school I _____ at the ice cream shop.

Down

1. What time does school _____ ?

3. Let's _____ up all the toys.

Review: Story Code

Crack the code by writing the correct review word in each blank. Write the word that goes with each symbol in the box below.

We're going to the library _____. I need to get an early
&

_____. My friend will _____ me up at _____ o' clock.
!   @

We need to _____ on a project for school.
*

I will _____ out about _____ books for us to read.
!   @

It's going to be a lot of _____. We won't finish the whole
*

project _____, but we will get a good _____!
&   #

_____

*   _____

&   _____

@   _____

!   _____

 **call**

say the word call aloud as you trace it.

call

Now practice writing the word once on each line.

_____
....
_____
....
_____
....
_____
....

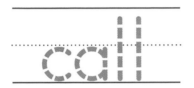

I like to _____ my friends on the phone.

Keep on Track

Look for the word **call** in each track. Circle it each time you see it. Then count the number of circled words in each track and write it in the sign.

c	a	l	c	a	l	l	a	l	l
c	a	l	l	c	a	l	l	c	a
c	l	l	a	c	l	c	a	l	l

cail call coll call call caul caal call

upon

say the word upon aloud as you trace it.

┆upon┆

Now practice writing the word once on each line.

Once _____ a time, there was an old king.

Word Watch

Circle the birds that have the word **upon** inside.

open

upon

upon

upon

upon

upen

upon

opon

upon

ubon

upun

full

say the word **full** aloud as you trace it.

full

Now practice writing the word once on each line.

WATER

The glass is _____.

What's the Order?

If the letters can be unscrambled to make the word **full**, write it on the line. If the letters don't make the word **full**, leave the line blank.

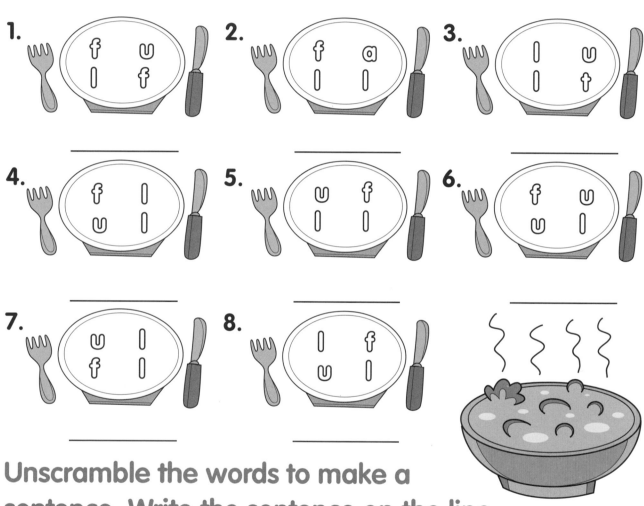

1. f u l f
   _____

2. f a l l
   _____

3. l u l t
   _____

4. f l u l
   _____

5. u f l l
   _____

6. f u u l
   _____

7. u l f l
   _____

8. l f u l
   _____

Unscramble the words to make a sentence. Write the sentence on the line.

bowl   The   very   full.   is

_____

say the word laugh aloud as you trace it.

laugh

Now practice writing the word once on each line.

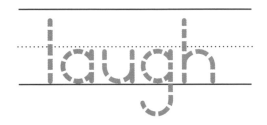

The clown makes me _____.

Stop and Go

Draw a line to connect the letters and make the word **laugh**.

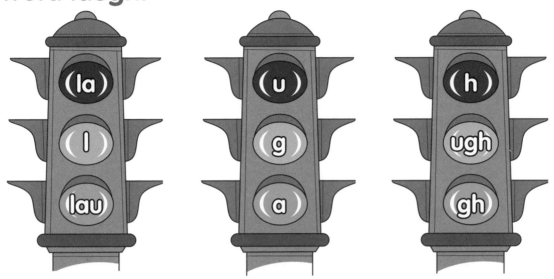

Fill in the blanks to complete the word laugh.

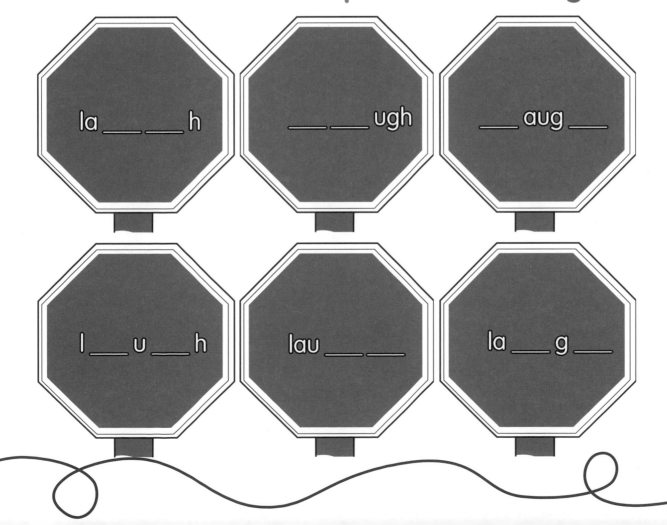

la ___ ___ h

___ ___ ___ ugh

___ aug ___

l ___ u ___ h

lau ___ ___ ___

la ___ g ___

say the word hold aloud as you trace it.

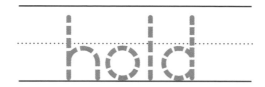

Now practice writing the word once on each line.

I like to _____ my baby sister.

Amazing Maze

Look for the word hold in the maze. Connect all the words that spell hold to find your way out of the maze.

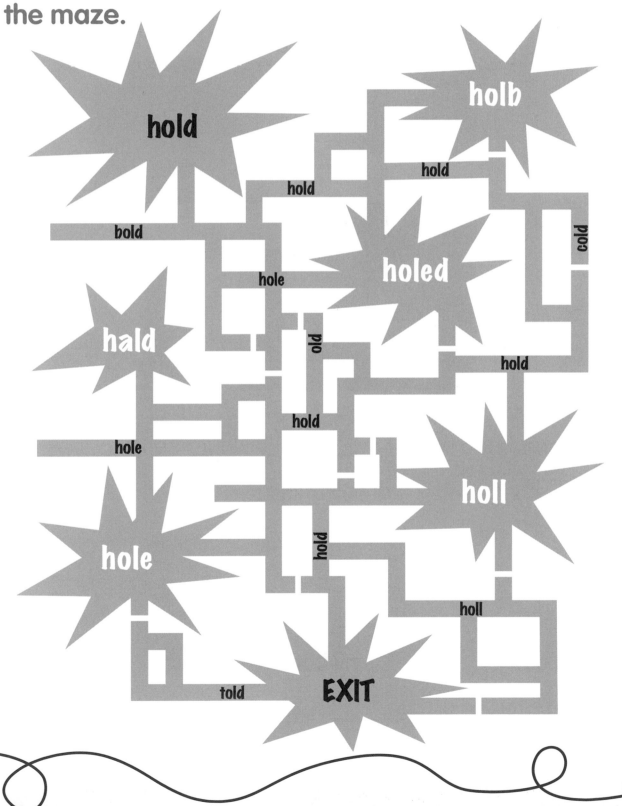

Review: Crossword Puzzle!

Use the sentence clues below to solve the crossword puzzle.

call   upon   full   laugh   hold

Across

2. Raise your hand when I _____ your name.

3. I always _____ at funny jokes.

Down

1. My pockets are _____ of coins.

4. I like to ride _____ my dad's shoulders.

5. Get in a circle and _____ hands.

Review: Story Code

Crack the code by writing the correct review word in each blank. Write the word that goes with each symbol in the box below.

Once _____ a time, there was a very funny boy. He liked
          #

to do tricks and make people _____ . People liked to
                              @

_____ him "the Joker." His magic bag was _____ of all
   &   !

his tricks. He never let anyone else _____ his magic bag.
                                      *

He had so many tricks that his bag got too _____. It was
                                            !

too heavy for the boy to _____ . He put his bag _____ a
                         *   #

horse. He decided to _____ his horse "Trick Trot." Trick Trot
                     &

and the Joker were good at making people _____ .
                                         @

```
#  _____
*  _____
&  _____
@  _____
!  _____
```

137

Review: ABC Gumballs

Write the review words in alphabetical order.

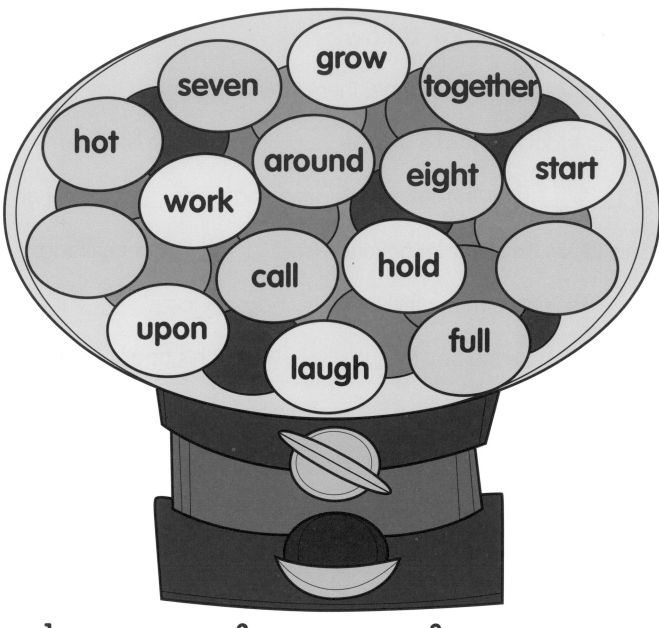

1. _____   2. _____   3. _____

4. _____   5. _____   6. _____

7. _____   8. _____   9. _____

10. _____ 11. _____ 12. _____

13. _____

Review: Sentence Squares

Read each group of sentences. Then find the group of words below that completes the sentences. Fill the missing words in the blanks.

1. _____ my parents are _____ thirsty, lemonade is _____ favorite thing to _____ .

2. I need to _____ my bedroom _____ on so I can _____ my report _____ tigers.

3. In art class _____ , I _____ to _____ my favorite color and _____ a picture.

today	draw
got	pick

about	keep
light	write

drink	If
their	both

Answer Key

Page 5

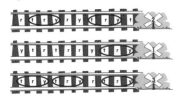

Page 7

Page 9

n	1: h	(s)	1: c	s	1: d
g	2: c	i	2: l	n	2: o
s	3: l	n	3: e	g	3: i
i	4: a	g	4: a	i	4: f
(s)	5: n	s	5: b	s	5: h
i	6: g	i	6: p	i	6: u
n	7: e	g	7: f	n	7: r
g	8: t	n	8: i	g	8: g
i	9: y	i	9: o	(s)	9: a
s	10: e	n	10: v	i	10: w
n	11: t	g	11: r	n	11: a
g	12: h	s	12: y	g	12: y

Why did the burglar take a shower?
He wanted to make a <u>clean</u>
<u>getaway</u>!

Page 11

<u>tent</u>
<u>tenth</u>
<u>tennis</u>
<u>tense</u>
<u>tend</u>
<u>pretend</u>

Page 13

Dear Alex,
I hope you can visit me this summer.
There are so many things for us to do.
My dad will make us pancakes every day.
Our tree house is big enough for us to
sleep in. You can stay with us as long as
you want!
Sincerely,
Justin
Inside box: 4

Dear Justin,
You've planned a lot of fun things
for us My parents want you to come
camping with us They will take us to the
mountains. There is a tent just for us Call
us and let us know if you can come.
Sincerely,
Alex
Inside box: 6

Page 14

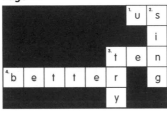

Page 15

Box 3 is checked.

Page 17

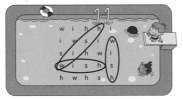

1. yes
2. no
3. no
4. yes
5. yes
6. no

Page 19

These letters can be unscrambled to make
the word **fast**:
1. fast
5. fast
6. fast
You ate your meal fast.

Page 21

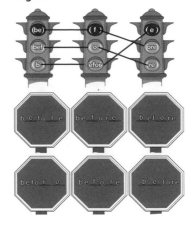

Page 23

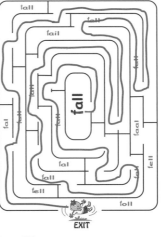

Page 25

1. I have never been to New York.
2. I told my mom I would never do it
again.
3. I never wake up on time.
4. The snow is something I have never
seen.
5. I would never tell a lie.
<u>growing</u> old

Page 26

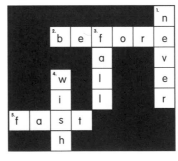

Page 27

My birthday <u>wish</u> was to go to the
lake. I had <u>never</u> been there <u>before.</u> My
<u>wish</u> came true. <u>Before</u> we left, my
brother said, "Be careful not to <u>fall</u> in
the lake!"
We got to the lake, and <u>before</u> anyone
could stop me, I ran to the water very
<u>fast</u>. I was running so <u>fast</u>, I fell into the
water.
"I knew you would <u>fall</u> in!" said my
brother.
I <u>wish</u> I had <u>never</u> gone to the lake!
wish
* never
& before
@ fall
! fast

Page 29

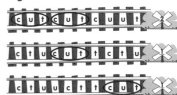

Page 31

Page 33

r	1: c	u	1: y	(h)	1: H
h	2: k	r	2: e	u	2: e
t	3: l	t	3: s	r	3: f
u	4: a	h	4: S	t	4: e
h	5: r	u	5: l	(s)	5: a
n	6: e	r	6: t	g	6: t
u	7: n	t	7: c	g	7: h
r	8: o	h	8: t	i	8: e
(h)	9: a	r	9: w	s	9: s
u	10: m	u	10: a	i	10: r
r	11: m	r	11: s	n	11: e
t	12: y	d	12: n	g	12: y

Why did the cookie go to the doctor?
<u>He felt crummy</u>!

Page 35
farm
farther
afar
farmer

Page 37
Dear Emily,
I can't go to the beach today because it's raining. Rainy days are nice because I can stay inside and write letters. I am excited because I can use my new pen. My dad gave it to me because I did well on my spelling test. I hope to become the best speller in my class! I study every night because I want to be in the spelling bee!
Sincerely,
Anna
Inside box: 5

Dear Anna,
I like getting your letters because they are always fun to read. I like rainy days too, but not because I can write letters. I like rainy days because I can read by the fire. Sometimes on rainy days I read old letters from my pen pals. I never throw away a letter because I might want to read it again. I keep all my letters in a box right beside my bed.
Sincerely,
Emily
Inside box: 4

Page 38
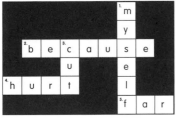

Page 39
Box 4 is checked.

Page 41
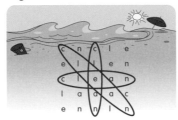

1. yes
2. no
3. no
4. no
5. yes
6. yes

Page 43
These letters can be unscrambled to make the word **much**:
3. much
4. much
5. much
7. much
How much do you want?

Page 45
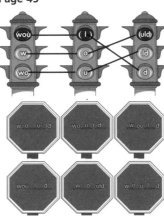

Page 47

Page 49
1. Please carry your plate to the sink.
2. My bag is too heavy to carry.
3. I like to carry my brother on my back.
4. There are too many books to carry.
5. I can't carry this to the car!
tall tale

Page 50
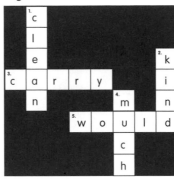

Page 51
   I have a very kind neighbor. She always helps us carry the groceries in from the car. My family likes her very much.
   One day, she asked if I would help her. She needed to clean out her garage. There was too much stuff for her to carry. I told her I would help her.
   When we were done, her garage was so clean! It felt good to do something kind for her.
kind
* would
& clean
@ much
! carry

Page 53

Page 55

Page 57

d 1: F	d 1: c	o 1: V
o 2: i	o 2: o	d 2: e
n 3: r	n 3: d	n 3: r
e 4: e	n 4: e	d 4: y
5: a	d 5: g	o 5: c
o 6: t	o 6: A	n 6: r
e 7: h	n 7: t	e 7: a
8: i	n 8: h	8: c
n 9: t	d 9: k	n 9: l
d 10: r	o 10: e	o 10: a
o 11: u	n 11: r	n 11: a
n 12: n	e 12: s	e 12: b

What do firemen put in their soup?
Fire crackers!

Page 59
longing
longer
lifelong
along
belong
longest

Page 61
Dear Noah,
Whenever I go on a trip, I always bring a pen and paper along. It's always fun to send you a letter about my trip. My family always camps at the same place every year. This year, the place we always go to is full. So we drove around until we found a new place to camp. I like the new place even better!
Sincerely,
Gabe
Inside box: 4

Dear Gabe,
I always like reading your letters. You always have a fun story to tell. My family always camps at the same place too. Whenever we camp, we always go on a hike. I wanted to go on the hike alone, but my parents wouldn't allow it. They said you should always hike with a buddy.
Sincerely,
Noah
Inside box: 5

Page 62

Page 63
Box 3 is checked.

Page 65

1. no
2. no
3. no
4. yes
5. yes
6. yes

Page 67
These letters can be unscrambled to make the word **which**:
1. which
2. which
5. which
6. which
Which one do you want?

Page 69

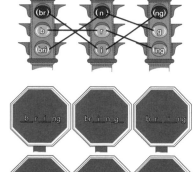

Page 71

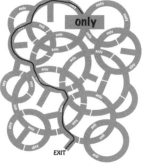

Page 73
1. This shirt is too (small).
2. A (small) bug was on the ground.
3. I would like to order a (small) drink.
4. I'm too (small) to go on that ride.
5. These shoes are too (small).
falling star

Page 74

Page 75
   What shall we do when Grandpa comes to visit? He will only be here for a few days. I told him to bring his favorite game. I wonder which game he will bring.
   Which room will Grandpa sleep in? My room is very small, and I only have one pillow. Grandpa says that my room is not too small for him. He will bring his own pillow. So, we shall be roommates!
shall
* bring
& which
@ only
! small

Page 76
1. before
2. cut
3. fall
4. far
5. fast
6. never
7. only
8. shall
9. sing
10. six
11. small
12. ten
13. which
14. wish
15. would

Page 77
1. When grandma comes to visit us, she likes to bring gifts. She has done this for a long time, and we like it very much.

2. My sister always does kind things.

Page 83

t	1: F	t	1: g		1: W
h	2: o	h	2: r	h	2: i
e	3: r	e	3: l	e	3: t
r	4: e	r	4: b	i	4: h
e	5: h	e	5: n		5: t
t	6: o	n	6: t	h	6: e
h	7: m	h	7: k	e	7: r
e	8: a	e	8: o	i	8: s
i	9: i	r	9: a		9: l
t	10: o	e	10: d	t	10: a
h	11: a		11: p	h	11: r
e	12: n	h	12: a	e	12: b
i	13: d	e	13: s	i	13: r
t	14: g	i	14: t		14: a
e	15: o		15: e	e	15: d

How do you repair a broken tomato?
With tomato paste!

Page 85
slight
lightning
flight
stoplight
lighthouse
sunlight

Page 87
Dear Bonnie,
I wonder (if) we can see each other this summer. Do you know (if) you are taking a summer vacation? It would be fun to see you (if) you are in my area. I will ask my parents (if) you can stay with us. (If) you want, we can sleep in a tent in my backyard.
Sincerely,
Betty
Inside box: 5

Dear Betty,
I will ask my parents (if) I can come to visit you. I'm sure that (if) we are in your area, it will be okay. It would be fun to sleep in a tent (if) it's not too cold. I've always wanted to do that! (If) we talk to our parents about it, I bet they will say yes!
Sincerely,
Bonnie
Inside box: 4

Page 88

Page 89
Box 1 is checked.

Page 91

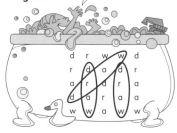

1. yes
2. no
3. no
4. yes
5. no
6. yes

Page 93
These letters can be unscrambled to make the word **seven**:
3. seven
4. seven
5. seven
8. seven
There are seven slices of pie.

Page 95

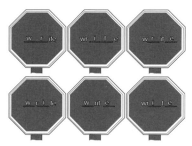

Page 97
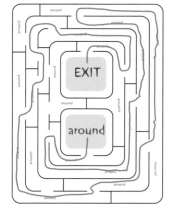

Page 99
1. Tell me all about yourself.
2. I don't know what that movie is about.
3. Talk about your summer plans.
4. I need to write a report about robots.
5. We learned about animals at the zoo.
square dance

Page 100

¹a	r	o	u	n	²d	³s
b					r	e
o					a	v
u				⁴w	r	i	t	e
t						n

Page 101
When I was <u>seven</u> years old, we moved to a new town. I was sad <u>about</u> moving. My friends gathered <u>around</u> to say goodbye. We said we would <u>write</u> letters.

Our new house was so big, it had <u>seven</u> bedrooms. We had a big yard where our dog could run <u>around</u>. I didn't forget to <u>write</u> my friends and tell them <u>about</u> our new house. They wrote back and asked me to <u>draw</u> a picture of my new house. It was fun to <u>draw</u> pictures and <u>write</u> my friends letters.
about
* around
& write
@ seven
! draw

Page 103

Page 105

Page 107

b	1: a	b	1: A	b	1: d
o	2: g	o	2: j	a	2: o
o	3: i	t	3: e	t	3: n
t	4: f		4: l	h	4: v
h	5: W	b	5: p	b	5: l
b	6: a	o	6: r	o	6: y
o	7: y	h	7: i	t	7: b
t	8: l	t	8: t		8: u
b	9: t	d	9: y	o	9: T
o	10: t	o	10: e	t	10: h
o	11: o	t	11: d	h	11: i
t	12: n	h	12: s	b	12: r

What's in the middle of a jellyfish?
<u>A jelly button!</u>

Page 109
<u>grown</u>
<u>grow</u>th
out<u>grow</u>
<u>grow</u>ing

Page 111
Dear Jake,
I can't wait to get ⟨together⟩ this weekend. I've planned lots of fun things for us to do ⟨together⟩ We can play in the backyard ⟨together⟩ I like to gather up all the leaves and make a big pile. ⟨Together⟩ we can make the biggest pile ever! See you soon!
Sincerely,
Steve
Inside box: 4

Dear Steve,
We always have fun when we're ⟨together⟩ My dad and I will ride ⟨together⟩ on the train to get to your house. We will play games ⟨together⟩ to pass the time. I'll bring my basketball with me. Maybe we can get ⟨together⟩ a group to play basketball. I'm excited to spend time ⟨together⟩
Sincerely,
Jake
Inside box: 5

Page 112

¹g					
o				²k	
³t	o	g	e	t	h	e	r
		r		e	
	⁵b	o	t	h	p
	w				

Page 113
Box 1 is checked.

Page 115

1. yes
2. yes
3. yes
4. no
5. no
6. no

Page 117
These letters can be unscrambled to make the word **eight**:
4. eight
5. eight
6. eight
7. eight
I drank eight glasses of milk.

Page 119
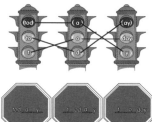

Page 121

Page 123

1. Don't start the game without me.
2. When does the movie start?
3. Wash your hands before you start.
4. Start the timer now, please.
5. You can start first, and I'll go next.

highchair

Page 124

Page 125

We're going to the library today. I need to get an early start. My friend will pick me up at eight o' clock. We need to work on a project for school.

I will pick out about eight books for us to read. It's going to be a lot of work. We won't finish the whole project today, but we will get a good start!

start
* work
& today
@ eight
! pick

Page 127

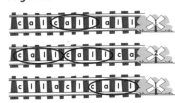

Page 129

Page 131

These letters can be unscrambled to make the word **full**:

4. full
5. full
7. full
8. full
The bowl is very full.

Page 133

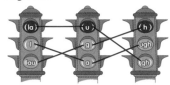

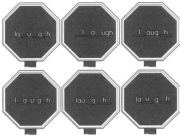

Page 135

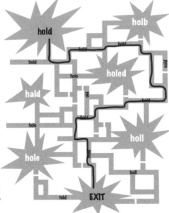

Page 136

Page 137

Once upon a time, there was a very funny boy. He liked to do tricks and make people laugh. People liked to call him "the Joker." His magic bag was full of all his tricks. He never let anyone else hold his magic bag.

He had so many tricks that his bag got too full. It was too heavy for the boy to hold. He put his bag upon a horse. He decided to call his horse "Trick Trot." Trick Trot and the Joker were good at making people laugh.

upon
* hold
& call
@ laugh
! full

Page 138

1. around
2. call
3. eight
4. full
5. grow
6. hold
7. hot
8. laugh
9. seven
10. start
11. together
12. upon
13. work

Page 139

1. If my parents are both thirsty, lemonade is their favorite thing to drink.

2. I need to keep my bedroom light on so I can write my report about tigers.

3. In art class today, I got to pick my favorite color and draw a picture.